Vibrant & Tasty Dash Diet Slow Cooker Cooking Guide

Need New Recipes? Try This Innovative Cookbook

Carmela Rojas

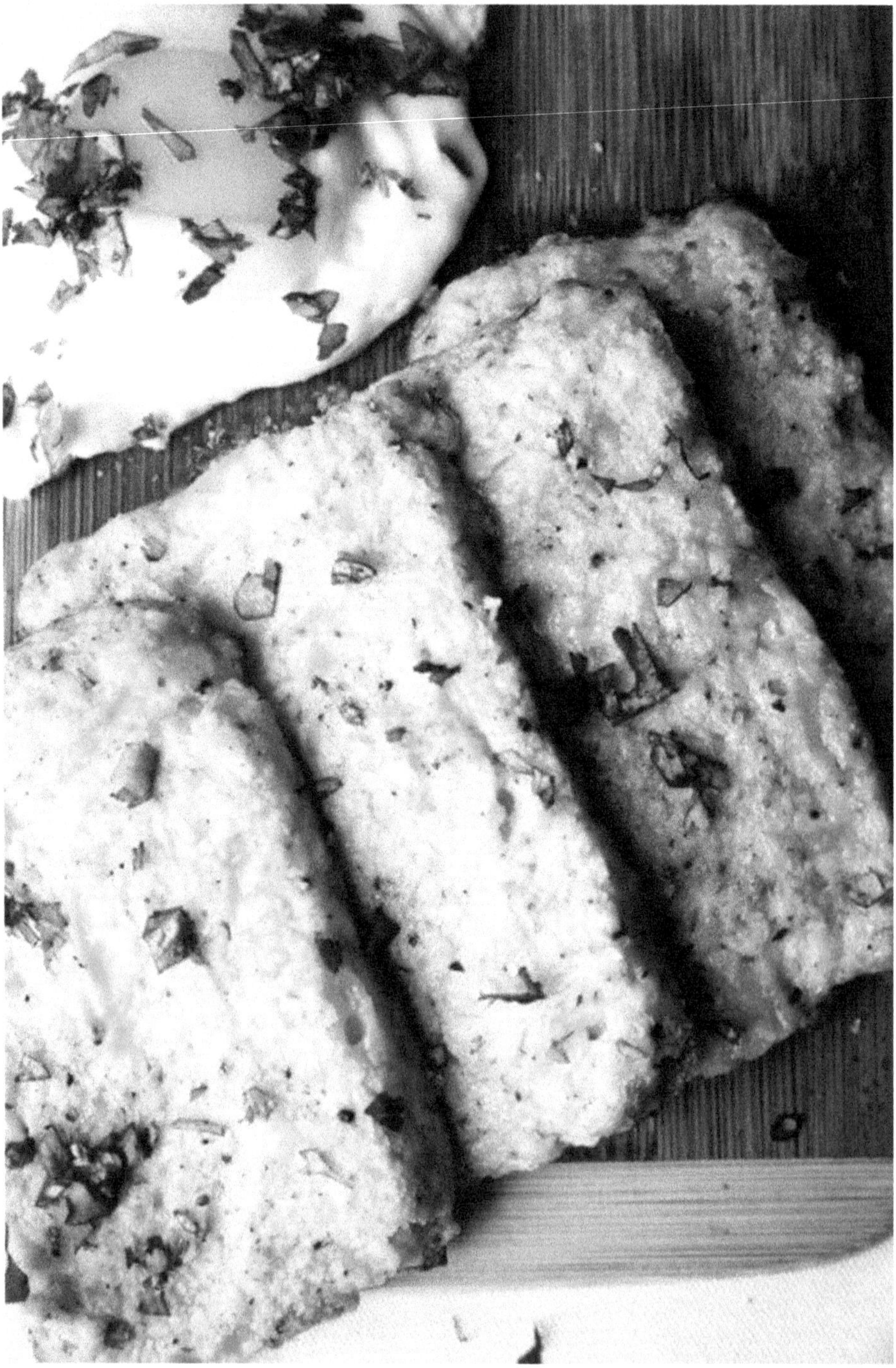

indirect, which are incurred as a result of the use of information contained within this document, including, but not limited to, — errors, omissions, or inaccuracies.

TABLE OF CONTENTS

Jalapeno Hash Browns

Servings: 4

Cooking Time: 3 Hours

Ingredients:
- 1 pound hash browns
- 1 and ½ cups low-sodium sausage, sliced
- ¼ cup spring onions, chopped
- 1 cup cherry tomatoes, halved
- 1 cup low-sodium veggie stock
- 1 jalapeno, chopped
- A pinch of black pepper

Directions:
1. In the slow cooker, combine the hash browns with the sausage and the other ingredients, put the lid on and cook on High for 3 hours.
2. Divide into bowls and serve.

Nutrition Info:

Calories 315, Fat 14.3g, Cholesterol 0mg, Sodium 489mg, Carbohydrate 43.3g, Fiber 4.4g, Sugars 4.3g, Protein 4g, Potassium 785mg

Caramel Bread Pudding

Servings: 12 Servings

Ingredients:

- 12 ounces (340 g) sweet bread, like challah or Hawaiian
- 4 cups (950 ml) skim milk
- ½ cup (100 g) sugar
- ¾ cup (175 ml) egg substitute
- 1 teaspoon vanilla
- 1 cup (225 g) caramel ice cream topping

Directions:

1. Cube bread and place in slow cooker. Whisk together remaining ingredients except caramel topping. Pour over bread. Press bread down into mixture. Cover and refrigerate at least 4 hours. Cover and cook on low 7 to 8 hours. Drizzle topping over to serve.

Nutrition Info:

Per serving: 106 g water; 220 calories (7% from fat, 15% from protein, 78% from carb); 8 g protein; 2 g total fat; 0 g saturated fat; 1 g monounsaturated fat; 1 g polyunsaturated fat; 44 g carb; 2 g fiber; 11 g sugar; 174 mg phosphorus; 166 mg calcium; 1 mg iron; 310 mg sodium; 283 mg potassium; 248 IU vitamin A; 57 mg ATE vitamin E; 1 mg vitamin C; 2 mg cholesterol

Crunchy Pears

Servings: About 3

Cooking Time: 2 Hrs 10 Mins

Ingredients:

- 2 ½ cups chopped Pear
- ½ tbsp. Lemon Juice
- 1 tbsp. Maple Syrup
- ¼ tsp. Nutmeg (grated)
- 1 tsp. Cornstarch
- ½ cup Granola (homemade)
- Canola Oil

Directions:

1. Coat the slow cooker with canola oil.
2. Place all the ingredients in the cooker.
3. Cook on "low" for 2 hrs.
4. Sprinkle on the Granola and leave it for 10 mins.
5. Serve hot.

Nutrition Info:

(Estimated Amount Per Serving): 201 Calories; 0 g Total Fats; 7 mg Sodium; 0 mg Cholesterol; 38 g Carbohydrates; 6 g Dietary Fiber; 4 g Protein

Black Beans Casserole

Servings: 8

Cooking Time: 4 Hours

Ingredients:

- 2 garlic cloves, minced
- 3 egg whites
- 2 tablespoons whole wheat flour
- ¾ cup tomato passata
- 15 ounces canned black beans, drained and rinsed
- 8 ounces canned green chili peppers, chopped
- ½ cup green onions, chopped
- Cooking spray
- 1 cup low-fat cheddar cheese, grated
- 3 egg yolks
- A splash of hot pepper sauce
- ½ cup fat-free milk
- 1 tablespoon cilantro, chopped

Directions:

1. Grease your slow cooker with cooking spray and add beans, chili peppers, tomato passata, green onions, pepper sauce, salt, garlic and cheese.

2. In a bowl, beat egg whites with a mixer.

3. In a separate bowl, mix egg yolks with salt and flour and whisk well.

4. Add egg whites, milk and cilantro and whisk well again.Pour this over beans mix, spread well, cover and cook on Low for 4 hours.

5. Slice, divide between plates and serve for breakfast.

Nutrition Info:

Calories 381, Fat 8.9g, Cholesterol 94mg, Sodium 159mg, Carbohydrate 58.1g, Fiber 16.5g, Sugars 15g, Protein 21.6g, Potassium 1406mg

Cashew And Carrot Muffins

Servings: 4

Cooking Time: 3 Hours

Ingredients:

- 4 tablespoons cashew butter, melted
- 4 eggs, whisked
- ½ cup coconut cream
- 1 cup carrots, peeled and grated
- 4 teaspoons maple syrup
- ¾ cup coconut flour
- ½ teaspoon baking soda

Directions:

1. In a bowl, mix the cashew butter with the eggs, cream and the other ingredients, whisk well and pour into a muffin pan that fits the slow cooker.
2. Put the lid on, cook the muffins on High for 3 hours, cool down and serve.

Nutrition Info:

Calories 345, Fat 21.7g, Cholesterol 164mg, Sodium 247mg, Carbohydrate 28.6g, Fiber 10.7g, Sugars 6.7g, Protein 12.3g, Potassium 327mg

Peach Cobbler

Servings: 6 Servings

Ingredients:

- 4 cups fresh (680 g), or canned (888 g) sliced peaches
- ¼ cup (20 g) rolled oats
- 1/3 cup (42 g) Heart-Healthy Baking Mix
- ½ cup (100 g) sugar
- ½ cup (115 g) brown sugar
- ¼ teaspoon cinnamon
- ½ cup (120 ml) water, or reserved peach juice if using canned peaches

Directions:

1. Spray inside of slow cooker with nonstick cooking spray. Place peaches in slow cooker. In a bowl, mix together oats, baking mix, sugar, brown sugar, and cinnamon. When blended, stir in water or juice until well mixed. Spoon batter into cooker and stir into peaches, just until blended. Cover and cook on low 4 to 5 hours.

Nutrition Info:

Per serving: 167 g water; 245 calories (1% from fat, 4% from protein, 95% from carb); 2 g protein; 0 g total fat; 0 g saturated fat; 0 g monounsaturated fat; 0 g polyunsaturated fat; 62 g carb; 3 g fiber; 52 g sugar; 65 mg phosphorus; 53 mg calcium; 1 mg iron; 55 mg sodium; 297 mg potassium; 653 IU vitamin A; 5 mg ATE vitamin E; 6 mg vitamin C; 2 mg cholesterol

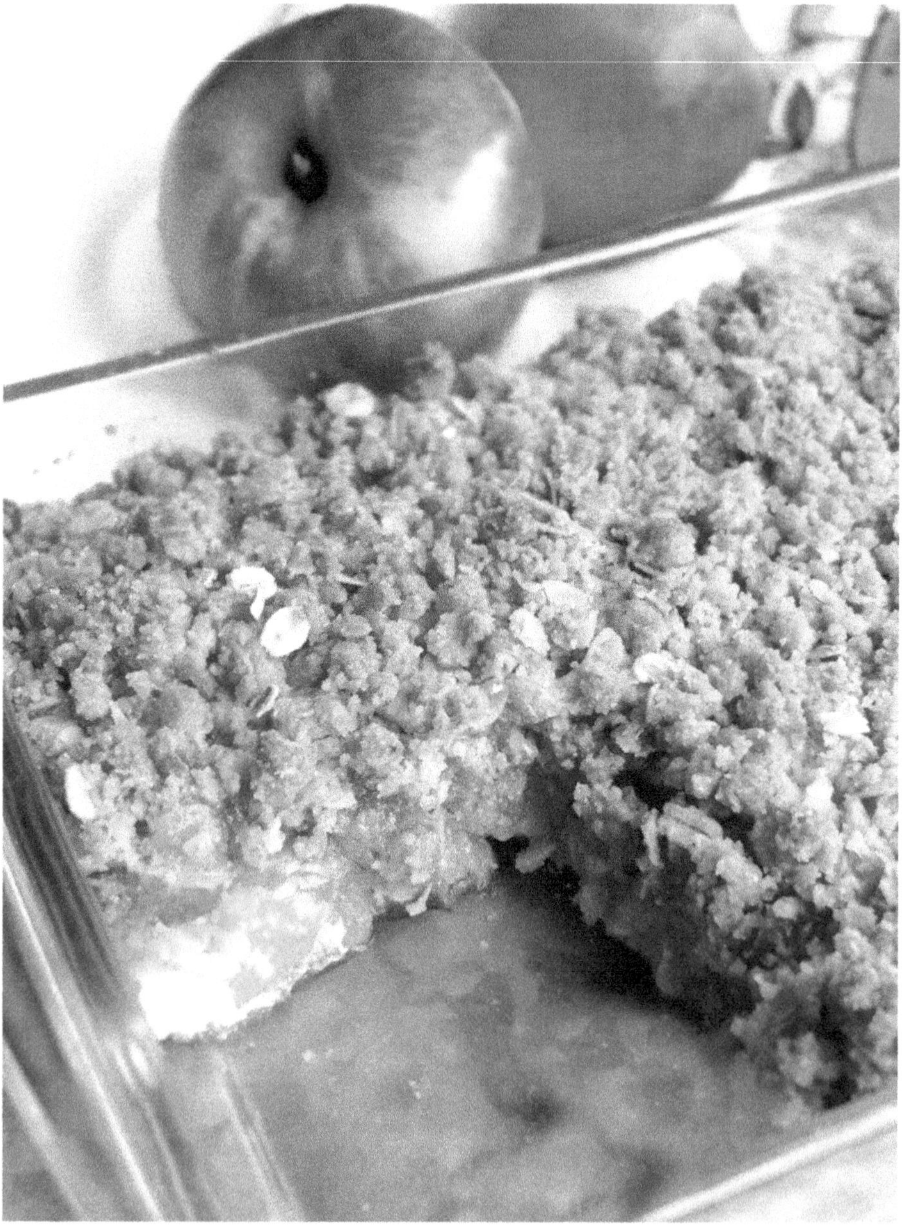

Cinnamon Fruit Dip

Servings: 4

Cooking Time: 3 Hours

Ingredients:

- 8 apples, cored and chopped
- 1 teaspoon cinnamon powder
- 2 drops cinnamon oil
- 1 cup water

Directions:

1. Put apples in your slow cooker, add the water, oil and cinnamon, cover, cook on High for 3 hours, blend using an immersion blender, divide into bowls and serve cold.

Nutrition Info:

Calories 297, Fat 7.8g, Cholesterol 0mg, Sodium 6mg, Carbohydrate 61.6g, Fiber 10.8g, Sugars 46.4g, Protein 1.2g, Potassium 478mg

Stevia Squash Breakfast Mix

Servings: 2

Cooking Time: 6 Hours

Ingredients:

- 1 big apple, cored, peeled and cut into wedges
- 2 teaspoons avocado oil
- 1 acorn squash, halved, deseeded and cubed
- 2 tablespoons stevia

Directions:

1. Grease your slow cooker with the oil, add apple, squash and stevia, toss, cover and cook on Low for 6 hours.
2. Divide into bowls and serve for breakfast.

Nutrition Info:

Calories 150, Fat 1g, Cholesterol 0mg, Sodium 8mg, Carbohydrate 53.1g, Fiber 6.1g, Sugars 11.6g, Protein 2.1g, Potassium 882mg

Apricot Custard

Servings: 10

Cooking Time: 3 Hours

Ingredients:

- 2 pounds apricots, chopped
- 2 tablespoons lemon juice
- 4 cups coconut sugar
- 1 teaspoon cinnamon powder
- 1 teaspoon vanilla extract

Directions:

1. In your slow cooker, mix the apricots with the sugar, lemon juice, cinnamon and vanilla, cover, cook on Low for 3 hours, blend using an immersion blender, divide into bowls and serve cold.

Nutrition Info:

Calories 83, Fat 0.6g, Cholesterol 0mg, Sodium 18mg, Carbohydrate 17.7g, Fiber 1.8g, Sugars 8.3g, Protein 1.6g, Potassium 239mg

Spicy Tomato Hash

Servings: 4

Cooking Time: 4 Hours

Ingredients:

- 1 pound hash browns
- 2 spring onions, chopped
- 1 cup cherry tomatoes, halved
- 4 eggs, whisked
- A pinch of cayenne pepper
- ½ cup low-sodium veggie stock
- 1 tablespoon cilantro, chopped

Directions:

1. In the slow cooker, combine the hash browns with the eggs and the other ingredients, put the lid on and cook on Low for 4 hours.
2. Divide the hash into bowls and serve right away for breakfast.

Nutrition Info:

Calories 376, Fat .18.7g, Cholesterol 164mg, Sodium 502mg, Carbohydrate 43g, Fiber 4.4g, Sugars 3.5g, Protein 9.5g, Potassium 842mg

Lemon Custard

Servings: 4

Cooking Time: 1 Hour

Ingredients:

- Juice of 2 lemons
- Zest of 2 lemons, grated
- 1 cup low-fat cream cheese
- ½ teaspoon vanilla extract
- 2 tablespoons coconut sugar
- 1 and ½ cups coconut cream

Directions:

1. In the slow cooker, combine the cream cheese with the lemon juice, zest and the other ingredients, put the lid on and cook on High for 1 hour.
2. Divide the cream into bowls and serve cold.

Nutrition Info:

Calories 324, Fat 22.4g, Cholesterol 5mg, Sodium 350mg, Carbohydrate 21.8g, Fiber 3.2g, Sugars 4.4g, Protein 11.4g, Potassium 390mg

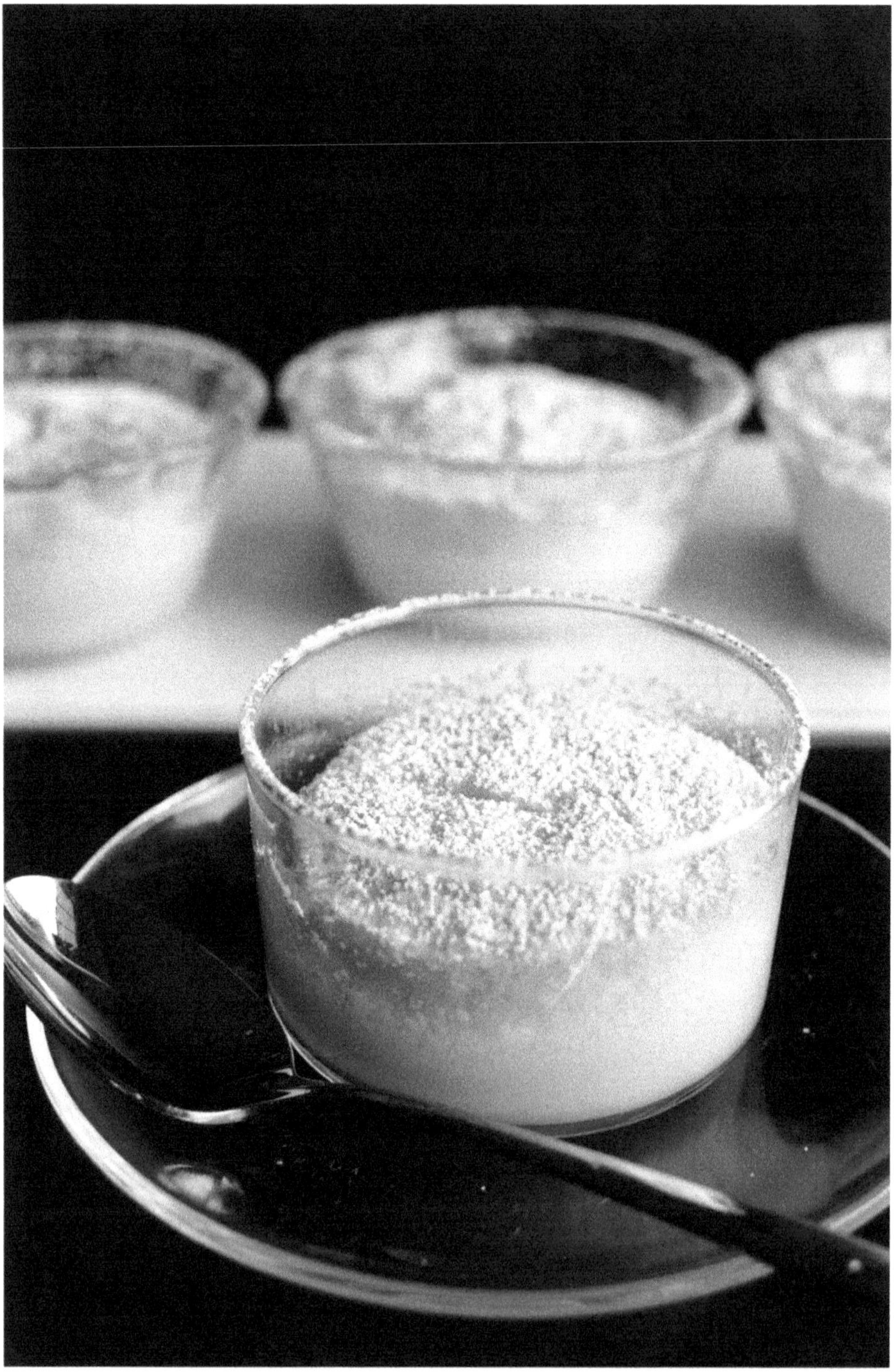

Chicken And Tomato Omelet

Servings: 2

Cooking Time: 3 Hours

Ingredients:

- 1-ounce rotisserie chicken, shredded
- 1 tomato, chopped
- 1 teaspoon mustard
- 1 tablespoon avocado mayonnaise
- 1 small avocado, pitted, peeled and chopped
- Black pepper to the taste
- 4 eggs, whisked

Directions:

1. In a bowl, mix the eggs with chicken, avocado, tomato, mayo and mustard, toss, transfer to your slow cooker, cover, cook on Low for 3 hours, divide between plates and serve.

Nutrition Info:

Calories 475, Fat 38g, Cholesterol 348mg, Sodium 800mg, Carbohydrate 19.9g, Fiber 7.6g, Sugars 6.6g, Protein 17.6g, Potassium 690mg

Coconut Sugar Compote

Servings: 4

Cooking Time: 2 Hours

Ingredients:

- 1 cup water
- 1 cup blackberries
- 1 cup strawberries, halved
- 1 cup blueberries
- ¼ cup coconut sugar
- Juice of 1 lime
- 2 teaspoons vanilla extract

Directions:

1. In your slow cooker, mix the berries with the water, sugar and the other ingredients, put the lid on and cook on Low for 2 hours.
2. Divide into bowls and serve cold.

Nutrition Info:

Calories 62, Fat 0.4g, Cholesterol 0mg, Sodium 6mg, Carbohydrate 13.9g, Fiber 3.6g, Sugars 7.6g, Protein 1.1g, Potassium 158mg

Blueberries Oatmeal

Servings: 4

Cooking Time: 2 Hours

Ingredients:

- 2 cups non-fat milk
- 1 cup old fashioned oats
- 1 cup blueberries
- 2 teaspoons sugar
- ½ teaspoon cinnamon powder
- ½ teaspoon vanilla extract
- ½ teaspoon almond extract

Directions:

1. In your slow cooker, combine the oats with the milk, berries and the other ingredients, put the lid on and cook on High for 2 hours.
2. Divide the oatmeal into bowls and serve for breakfast.

Nutrition Info:

Calories 231, Fat .2.7g, Cholesterol 2mg, Sodium 65mg, Carbohydrate 40.2g, Fiber 4.8g, Sugars 12.7g, Protein 9.3g, Potassium 391mg

Apple with Oatmeal

Servings: About 8

Cooking Time: 10 Hrs 15 Mins

Ingredients:

- 2 cups dry Oats (steel cut)
- 2 cups chopped Apples
- 1 cup of dried Cranberries (sweetened)
- 3 cup Water
- 1 cup Milk (low fat)
- 1 tbsp. ground Cinnamon
- 1 tsp. Pie Spice (pumpkin)
- 2 tsp. Margarine
- ½ cup o sliced Almonds
- ½ cup Pecans

Directions:

1. Place margarine in the cooker.
2. Except nuts, place all the ingredients into the cooker.
3. On "warm" setting, cook for 10 hrs. Serve with nuts

Nutrition Info:

(Estimated Amount Per Serving): 264.5 Calories; 7.1 g Total Fat; 1.5 Cholesterol; 28.7 mg Sodium; 47.8 mg Carbohydrates; 6.9 g Dietary Fiber; 8.4 g Protein

Cranberry Applesauce

Servings: 6 Servings

Ingredients:

- 6 apples, peeled or unpeeled, cut into 1-inch (2.5 cm) cubes
- ½ cup (120 ml) apple juice
- ½ cup (55 g) fresh cranberries
- ¼ cup (50 g) sugar
- ¼ teaspoon cinnamon

Directions:

1. Combine all ingredients in slow cooker. Cover and cook on low 3 to 4 hours or until apples are as soft as you like them. Serve warm or refrigerate and serve chilled.

Nutrition Info:

Per serving: 136 g water; 108 calories (2% from fat, 1% from protein, 97% from carb); 0 g protein; 0 g total fat; 0 g saturated fat; 0 g monounsaturated fat; 0 g polyunsaturated fat; 28 g carb; 2 g fiber; 24 g sugar; 17 mg phosphorus; 10 mg calcium; 0 mg

iron; 2 mg sodium; 149 mg potassium; 54 IU vitamin A; 0 mg
ATE vitamin E; 6 mg vitamin C; 0 mg cholesterol

Cinnamon And Allspice Dip

Servings: 20

Cooking Time: 3 Hours

Ingredients:

- 2 apples, cored and chopped
- 3 pounds plums, pitted and chopped
- 4 tablespoons cinnamon powder
- 4 tablespoons allspice, ground
- 4 tablespoons ginger, ground
- ¾ pound coconut sugar

Directions:

1. Put plums and apples in your slow cooker, add ginger, cinnamon, allspice and sugar, stir, cover and cook on High for 3 hours.
2. Pulse using an immersion blender, divide into bowls and serve.

Nutrition Info:

Calories 27, Fat 0.2g, Cholesterol 0mg, Sodium 3mg, Carbohydrate 6.6g, Fiber 1.1g, Sugars 3.4g, Protein 0.4g, Potassium 66mg

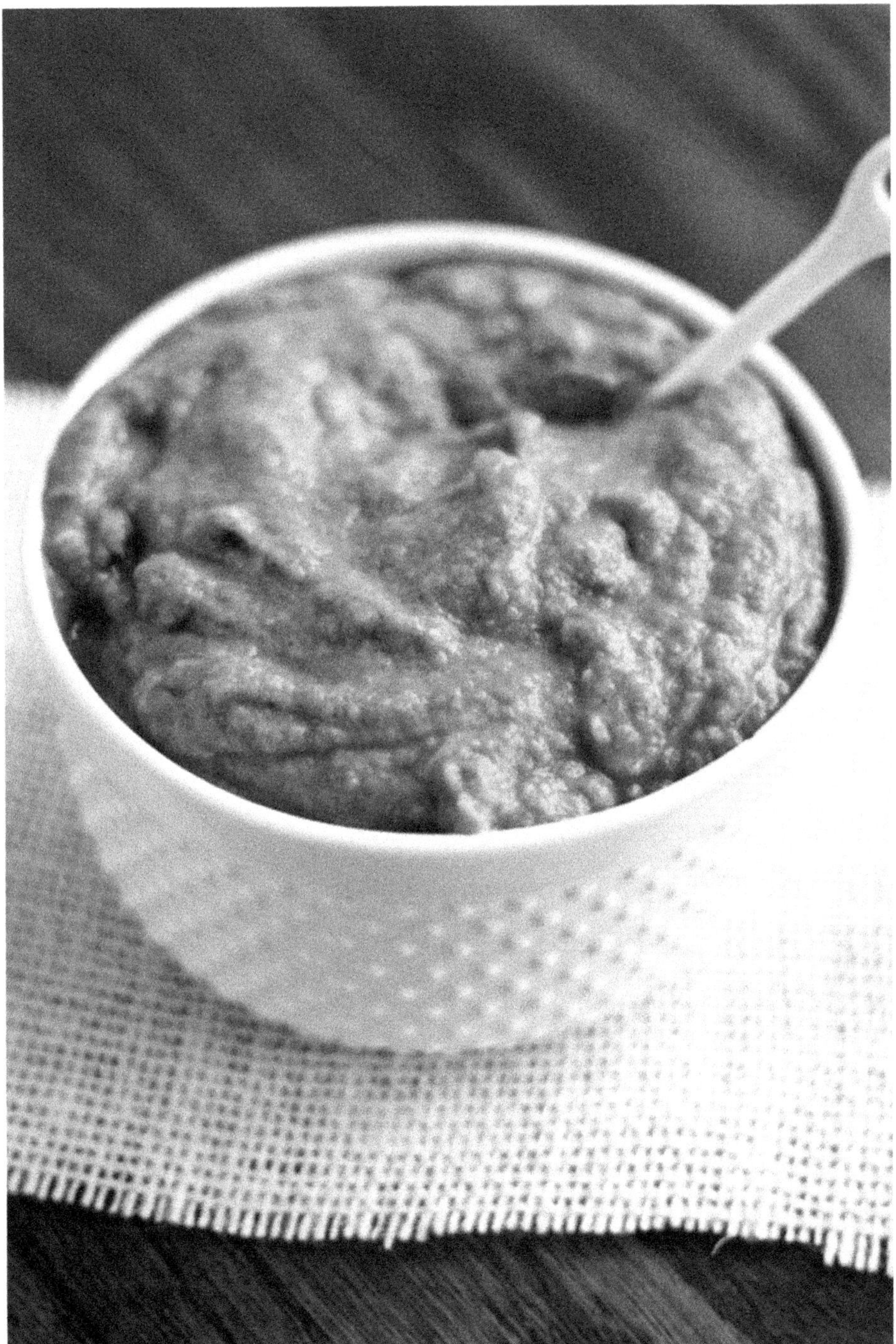

Spices And Zucchini Pie

Servings: 6

Cooking Time: 4 Hours

Ingredients:

- 1 cup natural applesauce
- 2 cups zucchini, grated
- 3 eggs, whisked
- 1 tablespoon vanilla extract
- 4 tablespoons stevia
- Cooking spray
- 2 and ½ cups coconut flour
- ½ cup baking cocoa powder
- 1 teaspoon cinnamon powder
- 1 teaspoon baking soda
- ¼ teaspoon baking powder

Directions:

1. Grease your slow with cooking spray, add zucchini, sugar, vanilla, eggs, applesauce, flour, cocoa powder, baking soda, baking powder and cinnamon, whisk, cook on High for 4 hours, cool down, slice and serve.

Nutrition Info: Calories 286, Fat 10.1g, Cholesterol 82mg, Sodium 350mg, Carbohydrate 42.5g, Fiber 18.7g, Sugars 7.9g, Protein 11g, Potassium 153mg

Cinnamon Pudding

Servings: 4

Cooking Time: 5 Hours

Ingredients:

- 2 cups white rice
- 1 cup coconut sugar
- 2 cinnamon sticks
- 6 and ½ cups water
- ½ cup coconut, shredded

Directions:

1. In your slow cooker, mix water with the rice, sugar, cinnamon and coconut, stir, cover, cook on High for 5 hours, discard cinnamon, divide pudding into bowls and serve warm.

Nutrition Info:

Calories 400, Fat 4g, Cholesterol 0mg, Sodium 28mg, Carbohydrate 81.2g, Fiber 2.7g, Sugars 0.8g, Protein 7.2g, Potassium 151mg

Cardamom Pears

Servings: 4

Cooking Time: 4 Hours

Ingredients:

- 5 cardamom pods
- 2 cups apple juice
- 4 pears, peeled and tops cut off and cored
- 1-inch ginger, grated
- ¼ cup maple syrup

Directions:

1. Put the pears in your slow cooker, add cardamom, apple juice, maple syrup and ginger, cover, cook on Low for 4 hours, divide into bowls and serve.

Nutrition Info:

Calories 241, Fat 0.7g, Cholesterol 0mg, Sodium 10mg, Carbohydrate 61.7g, Fiber 7.6g, Sugars 44.2g, Protein 1.2g, Potassium 454mg

Red Grape Compote

Servings: 2

Cooking Time: 4 Hours

Ingredients:

- 12 ounces red grape juice
- 1 cup maple syrup
- 2 cups green grapes, halved
- 1 cup water

Directions:

1. In your slow cooker, mix grapes with water, maple syrup and grape juice, stir, cover, cook on Low for 4 hours, divide into bowls and serve cold.

Nutrition Info:

Calories 593, Fat 0.6g, Cholesterol 0mg, Sodium 34mg, Carbohydrate 152.6g, Fiber 0.8g, Sugars 138.5g, Protein 0.6g, Potassium 498mg

Pepper And Cheese Frittata

Servings: 6

Cooking Time: 3 Hours

Ingredients:

- A pinch of black pepper
- 14 ounces small artichoke hearts, drained
- ¼ cup green onions, chopped
- 12 ounces roasted red peppers, chopped
- 4 ounces low-fat cheese, grated
- 8 eggs, whisked

Directions:

1. In your slow cooker, mix the eggs with the red peppers, artichokes, green onions and black pepper and whisk.
2. Spread the cheese all over, cover and cook on Low for 3 hours.
3. Slice, divide between plates and serve.

Nutrition Info:

Calories 201, Fat 12.2g, Cholesterol 238mg, Sodium 526mg, Carbohydrate 9g, Fiber 2.8g, Sugars 3.1g, Protein 14.2g, Potassium 203mg

Coconut Pudding

Servings: About 4

Cooking Time: 6 Hrs 10 Mins

Ingredients:

- 1/8 tsp. Salt
- ½ cup Rice (white)
- ½ quart Soy Milk
- ½ cup Sugar
- 1/16 cup Coconut (shredded)
- ¼ cup Margarine (Vegan)
- ½ tsp. Cinnamon

Directions:

1. Place all ingredients in the slow cooker.
2. Cook on "low" for 6 hrs. Serve.

Nutrition Info:

(Estimated Amount Per Serving): 357 Calories; 14 g Total Fats; 137 mg Sodium; 0 mg Cholesterol; 52 g Carbohydrates; 1.5 g Dietary Fiber; 6 g Protein

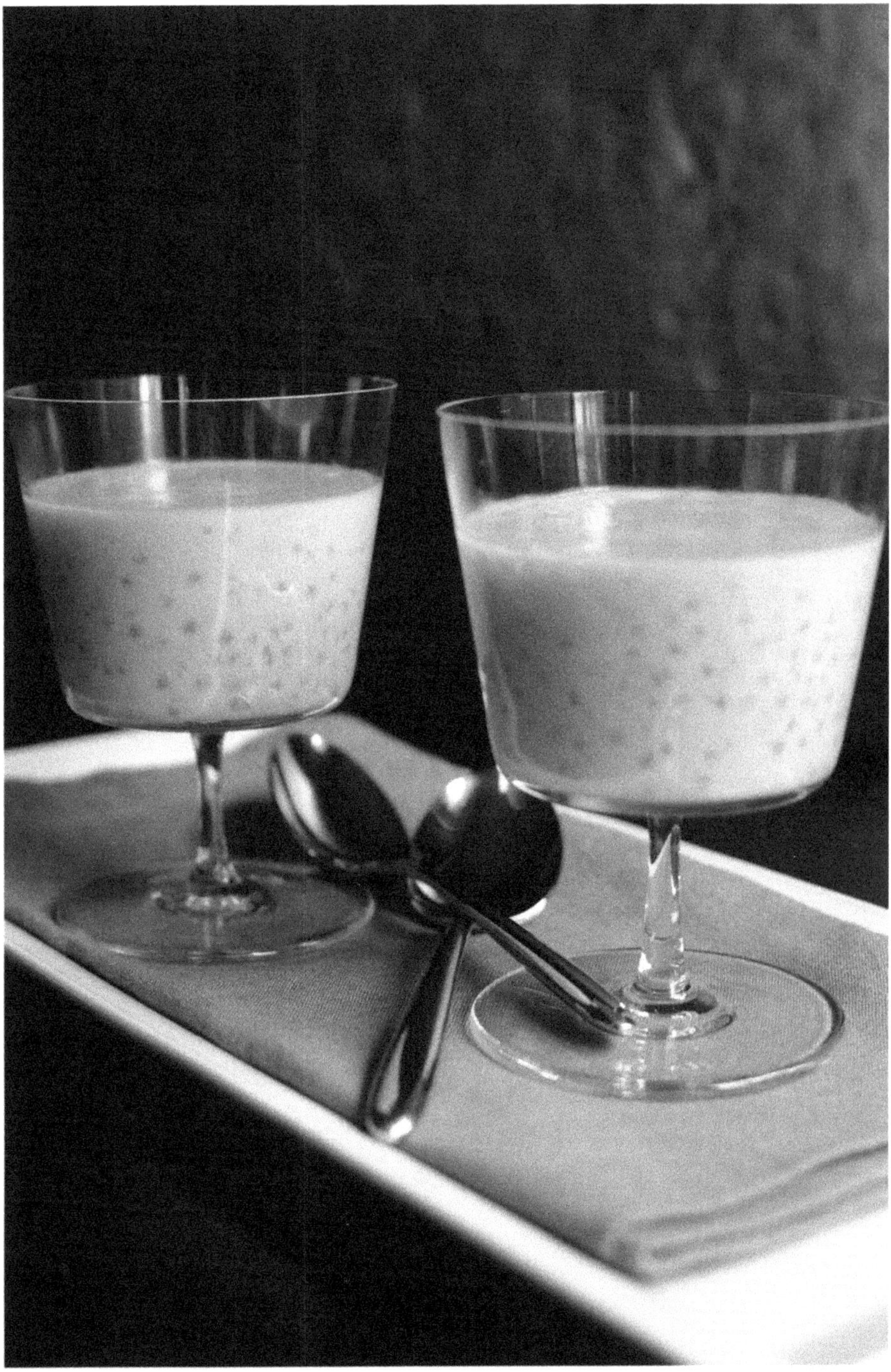

Bell Pepper And Sausage Pie

Servings: 4

Cooking Time: 8 Hours

Ingredients:

- 8 eggs, whisked
- 1 sweet potato, shredded
- 1 yellow onion, chopped
- 2 teaspoons basil, dried
- 2 teaspoons coconut oil, melted
- 1 tablespoon garlic powder
- 2 red bell peppers, chopped
- 1 pound sausage, crumbled
- Black pepper to the taste

Directions:

1. Grease your slow cooker with the oil; add sweet potatoes, sausage, garlic powder, bell pepper, onion, basil, salt and pepper.
2. Add the eggs, toss, cover, cook on Low for 8 hours, divide between plates and serve.

Nutrition Info:

Calories 625, Fat 44.9g, Cholesterol 423mg, Sodium 1266mg, Carbohydrate 19.4g, Fiber 2.7g, Sugars 9.5g, Protein 35.2g, Potassium 763mg

Sweet Chia Bowls

Servings: 4

Cooking Time: 2 Hours

Ingredients:

- 2 cups non-fat milk
- 1 cup brown rice
- 2 bananas, peeled and sliced
- 1 tablespoon maple syrup
- 2 tablespoons chia seeds
- 1teaspoon sugar
- 1 teaspoon vanilla extract
- 1 teaspoon cinnamon powder

Directions:

1. In your slow cooker, combine the milk with the bananas, maple syrup and the other ingredients, put the lid on and cook on High for 2 hours.
2. Divide the mix into bowls and serve for breakfast.

Nutrition Info:

Calories 321, Fat .3.5g, Cholesterol 3mg, Sodium 69mg, Carbohydrate 63.4g, Fiber 5.4g, Sugars 17.3g, Protein 9.3g, Potassium 577mg

Spiced Applesauce

Servings: 8 Servings

Ingredients:

- 4 pounds (1.8 kg) apples, pared, cored, and sliced
- ½ cup (100 g) sugar
- ½ teaspoon cinnamon
- 1 cup (235 ml) water
- 1 tablespoon (15 ml) lemon juice

Directions:

1. Place apples in slow cooker. Combine sugar and cinnamon and mix with apples. Blend in water and lemon juice. Cover and cook on low 5 to 7 hours or on high 2½ to 3½ hours.

Nutrition Info:

Per serving: 228 g water; 158 calories (2% from fat, 1% from protein, 97% from carb); 1 g protein; 0 g total fat; 0 g saturated fat; 0 g monounsaturated fat; 0 g polyunsaturated fat; 42 g carb; 3 g fiber; 36 g sugar; 25 mg phosphorus; 14 mg calcium; 0 mg iron; 1 mg sodium; 208 mg potassium; 87 IU vitamin A; 0 mg ATE vitamin E; 10 mg vitamin C; 0 mg cholesterol

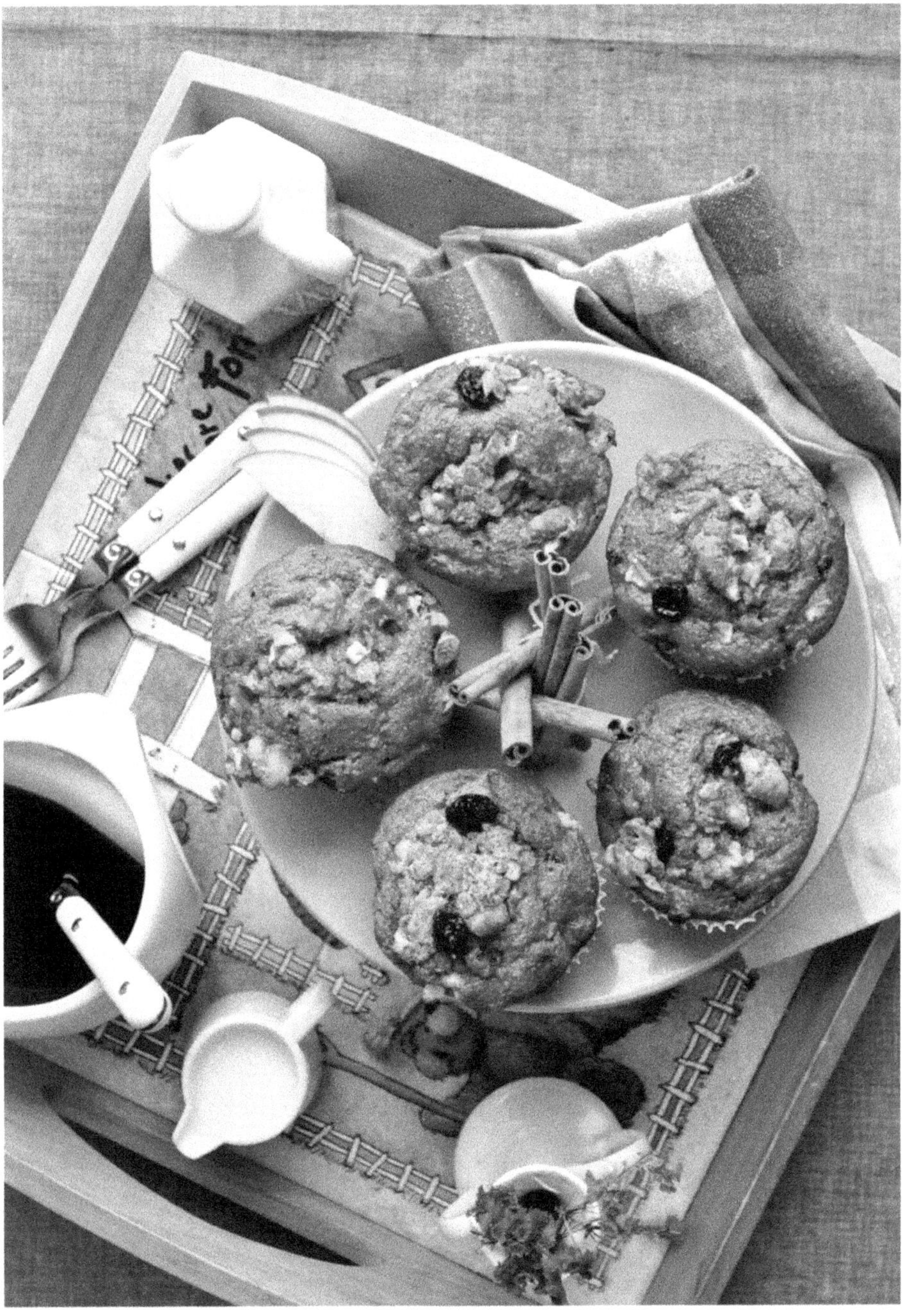

Eggs And Broccoli Casserole

Servings: 8

Cooking Time: 4 Hours

Ingredients:

- A pinch of black pepper
- 8 eggs
- 1 teaspoon garlic, minced
- ½ yellow onion, chopped
- 2 bell peppers, chopped
- ¾ cup low-fat milk
- 2 teaspoons mustard
- 1 small broccoli head, florets separated
- 30 ounces hash browns

Directions:

1. In a bowl, mix the eggs with the milk, mustard, garlic, hash browns, onion, bell peppers, broccoli and black pepper, stir, pour into your slow cooker, cover and cook on Low for 4 hours.
2. Divide between plates and serve.

Nutrition Info:

Calories 373, Fat .18.3g, Cholesterol 165mg, Sodium 438mg, Carbohydrate 42.5g, Fiber 4.2g, Sugars 5.1g, Protein 10.3g, Potassium 796mg

Basil Hash Bowls

Servings: 4

Cooking Time: 4 Hours

Ingredients:

- 1 pound hash browns
- 1 cup coconut cream
- 1 tablespoon oregano, chopped
- 1 tablespoon basil, chopped
- 1 teaspoon chili powder
- 1 teaspoon sweet paprika
- 6 eggs, whisked
- A pinch of cayenne pepper

Directions:

1. In your slow cooker, combine the hash browns with the cream, oregano and the other ingredients, put the lid on and cook on Low for 4 hours.
2. Divide between plates and serve for breakfast.

Nutrition Info:

Calories 540, Fat 35.4g, Cholesterol 246mg, Sodium 496mg, Carbohydrate 45.1g, Fiber 5.9g, Sugars 4.4g, Protein 13.4g, Potassium 946mg

Carrot Cake

Servings: 6

Cooking Time: 2 Hours And 30 Minutes

Ingredients:

- 1 cup pineapple, dried and chopped
- 4 carrots, chopped
- 1 cup dates, pitted and chopped
- ½ cup coconut flakes
- Cooking spray
- 1 and ½ cups whole wheat flour
- ½ teaspoon cinnamon powder

Directions:

1. Put carrots in your food processor and pulse.
2. Add flour, dates, pineapple, coconut, cinnamon, and pulse very well again.
3. Grease the slow cooker with the cooking spray, pour the cake mix, spread, cover and cook on High for 2 hours and 30 minutes.
4. Leave the cake to cool down, slice and serve.

Nutrition Info: Calories 252, Fat 2.8g, Cholesterol 0mg, Sodium 31mg, Carbohydrate 54.7g, Fiber 5.2g, Sugars 24g, Protein 4.7g, Potassium 412mg

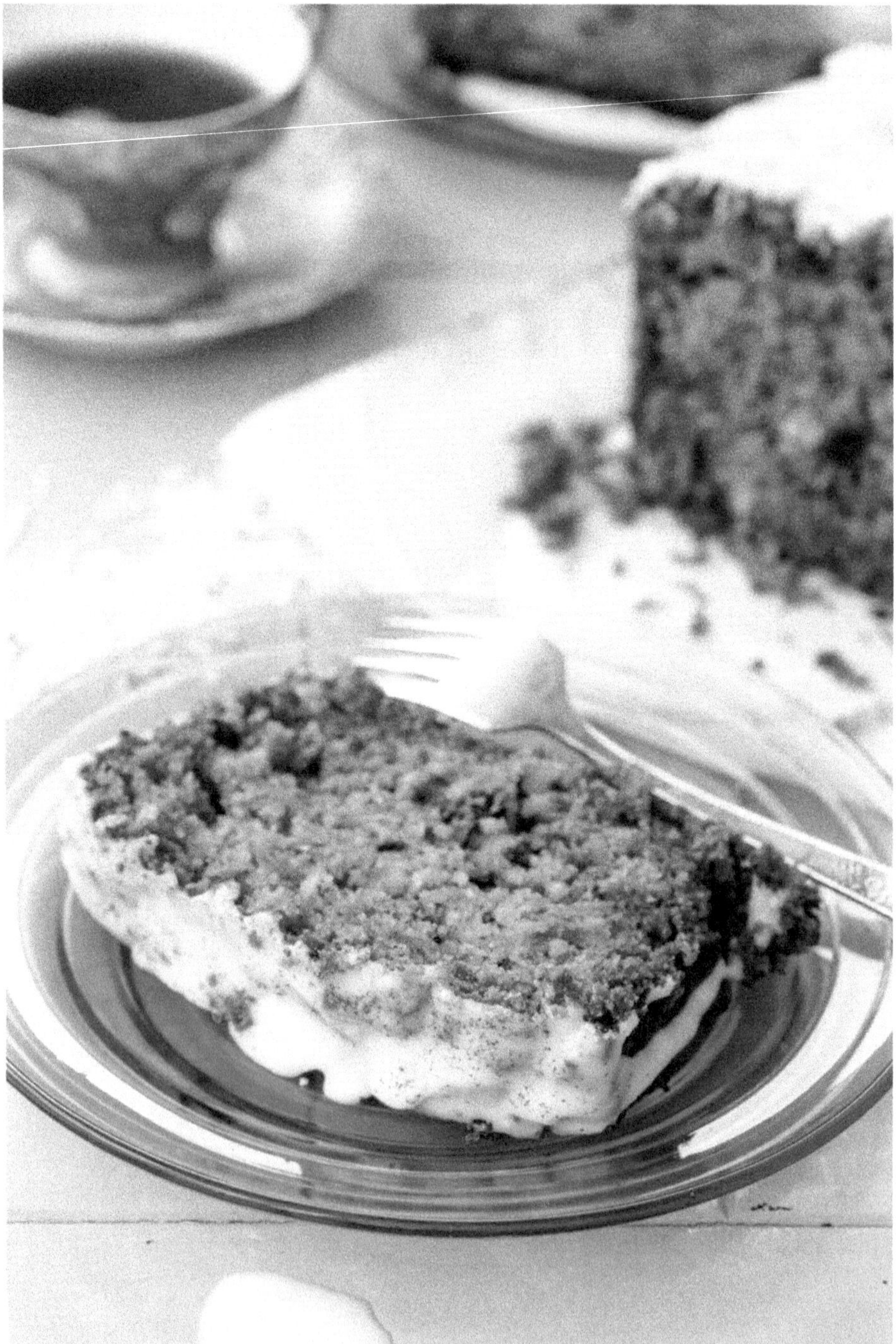

Resilient Chocolate Cream

Servings: 4

Cooking Time: 1 Hour And 30 Minutes

Ingredients:

- 1 cup dark and unsweetened chocolate, chopped
- ½ pound cherries, pitted and halved
- 1 teaspoon vanilla extract
- ½ cup coconut cream
- 3 tablespoons coconut sugar
- 2 teaspoons gelatin

Directions:

1. In the slow cooker, combine the chocolate with the cherries and the other ingredients, toss, put the lid on and cook on Low for 1 hour and 30 minutes.

2. Stir the cream well, divide into bowls and serve.

Nutrition Info:

Calories 526, Fat 39.9g, Cholesterol 0mg, Sodium 57mg, Carbohydrate 47.2g, Fiber 10.8g, Sugars 1.1g, Protein 13.4g, Potassium 141mg

Hot Spiced Fruit

Servings: 12 Servings

Ingredients:

- 1 pound (455 g) peaches canned in water, undrained
- 1 pound (455 g) pears canned in water, undrained
- 1 pound (455 g) pineapple canned in water, undrained
- 1 cup (250 g) stewed prunes
- ½ cup (160 g) orange marmalade
- 2 tablespoons (28 g) unsalted butter
- 1 stick cinnamon
- 1/8 teaspoon nutmeg
- 1/8 teaspoon ground cloves

Directions:

1. Drain liquid from all fruit, reserving 1½ cups (355 ml) to make syrup. Combine marmalade, butter, cinnamon stick, nutmeg, cloves, and reserved liquid in a saucepan. Bring to boil, then simmer 3 to 4 minutes. Cut fruit into chunks and gently add to saucepan. Transfer to slow cooker and cook on low at least 4 hours.

Nutrition Info:

Per serving: 116 g water; 130 calories (13% from fat, 2% from protein, 85% from carb); 1 g protein; 2 g total fat; 1 g saturated fat; 1 g monounsaturated fat; 0 g polyunsaturated fat; 30 g carb; 3 g fiber; 26 g sugar; 21 mg phosphorus; 21 mg calcium; 0 mg iron; 10 mg sodium; 205 mg potassium; 305 IU vitamin A; 16 mg ATE vitamin E; 7 mg vitamin C; 5 mg cholesterol

Strawberry Bread Pudding

Servings: 6 Servings

Ingredients:

- 5 cups (250 g) cubed French bread
- 2½ cups (570 ml) skim milk, scalded
- 2 egg yolks
- 1 cup (200 g) sugar
- 1 teaspoon vanilla
- 2 tablespoons (28 g) unsalted butter, melted
- 12 ounces (340 g) strawberries, at room temperature

Directions:

1. Place the bread cubes in the slow cooker. Whisk together the milk, egg yolks, sugar, vanilla, and butter. Stir in the berries and pour over the bread cubes. Gently press the bread down into the liquid (do not stir) and cook, covered, on low for 4 to 6 hours.

Nutrition Info:

Per serving: 170 g water; 410 calories (16% from fat, 12% from protein, 71% from carb); 13 g protein; 8 g total fat; 4 g saturated fat; 2 g monounsaturated fat; 1 g polyunsaturated fat; 74 g carb; 2 g fiber; 38 g sugar; 222 mg phosphorus; 190 mg calcium; 3 mg iron; 440 mg sodium; 367 mg potassium; 445 IU vitamin A; 124 mg ATE vitamin E; 35 mg vitamin C; 82 mg cholesterol

Broccoli And Garlic Omelet

Servings: 4

Cooking Time: 2 Hours

Ingredients:

- 1 red bell pepper, chopped
- Black pepper to the taste
- 1 cup broccoli florets
- A pinch of chili powder
- A pinch of garlic powder
- 1 yellow onion, chopped
- Cooking spray
- 6 eggs, whisked
- ½ cup low-fat milk
- 1 garlic clove, minced

Directions:

1. In a bowl, mix the eggs with the milk, black pepper, chili powder, garlic powder, red bell pepper, broccoli, onion and garlic and whisk well.
2. Grease your slow cooker with the cooking spray, spread the eggs mix on the bottom, cover and cook on High for 2 hours.

3. Slice the omelet, divide it between plates and serve.

Nutrition Info:

Calories 171, Fat 8.7g, Cholesterol 247mg, Sodium 396mg, Carbohydrate 13g, Fiber 1.8g, Sugars 7.5g, Protein 10.9g, Potassium 308mg

Rosemary Eggs With Pepppers

Servings: 4

Cooking Time: 2 Hours And 30 Minutes

Ingredients:

- 8 eggs, whisked
- 1 cup red roasted peppers, chopped
- 2 spring onions, chopped
- 1 teaspoon oregano, dried
- 1 teaspoon chili powder
- 1 teaspoon rosemary, dried
- ½ cup coconut cream
- A pinch of black pepper

Directions:

1. In the slow cooker, combine the eggs with the peppers, spring onions and the other ingredients, toss, put the lid on and cook on High for 2 hours and 30 minutes.
2. Divide the mix between plates and serve for breakfast.

Nutrition Info:

Calories 272, Fat .20.1g, Cholesterol 327mg, Sodium 816mg, Carbohydrate 11.7g, Fiber 1.4g, Sugars 7.9g, Protein 12g, Potassium 240mg

Cinnamon Peach Cobbler

Servings: 4

Cooking Time: 4 Hours

Ingredients:

- 4 cups peaches, peeled and sliced
- Cooking spray
- ¼ cup coconut sugar
- 1 and ½ cups whole wheat sweet crackers, crushed
- ½ cup almond milk
- ½ teaspoon cinnamon powder
- ¼ cup stevia
- 1 teaspoon vanilla extract
- ¼ teaspoon nutmeg, ground

Directions:

1. In a bowl, mix peaches with sugar, cinnamon, and stir.
2. In a separate bowl, mix crackers with stevia, nutmeg, almond milk and vanilla extract and stir.
3. Spray your slow cooker with cooking spray, spread peaches on the bottom, and add the crackers mix, spread, cover and cook on Low for 4 hours.

4. Divide into bowls and serve.

Nutrition Info:

Calories 249, Fat 11.4g, Cholesterol 0mg, Sodium 179mg, Carbohydrate 42.7g, Fiber 3g, Sugars 15.2g, Protein 3.5g, Potassium 366mg

Spiced Oatmeal

Servings: 4

Cooking Time: 9 Hours

Ingredients:

- 1 cup steel cut oats
- 2 tablespoons stevia
- ½ teaspoon cinnamon powder
- A pinch of cloves, ground
- ½ cup pumpkin puree
- 4 cups water
- Olive oil cooking spray
- ½ cup fat-free milk
- A pinch of nutmeg, ground
- A pinch of allspice, ground
- A pinch of ginger, ground

Directions:

1. Grease your slow cooker with the cooking spray, add the oats, the pumpkin puree, water, milk, stevia, cinnamon, cloves, allspice, ginger and nutmeg, cover and cook on Low for 9 hours.
2. Stir the oatmeal, divide it into bowls and serve.

Nutrition Info:

Calories 100, Fat 1.5g, Cholesterol 1mg, Sodium 26mg, Carbohydrate 25.5g, Fiber 3g, Sugars 2.7g, Protein 4g, Potassium 189mg

Banana And Almond Spread

Servings: 2

Cooking Time: 1 Hrs 10 Mins

Ingredients:

- 2 Bananas (large)

- 2 cups Almond Milk (unsweetened)

- 2 tbsp. Wheat Germ

- 2 tbsp. Almond Butter (unsalted)

- ¼ tsp. Cinnamon (ground)

- ¼ tsp. Vanilla Extract

- 6 Ice Cubes

Directions:

1. Puree all the ingredients in a blender.

2. Pour this puree in the slow cooker.

3. Cook on "low" for 1 hr.

4. Serve on Muffins or Bread.

Nutrition Info:

(Estimated Amount Per Serving): 338 Calories; 13 g Total Fats; 0 mg Cholesterol; 153 mg Sodium; 52 mg Carbohydrates; 8 g Dietary Fiber; 10 g Protein

Rice Pudding

Servings: 6 Servings

Ingredients:

- 2½ cups (413 g) cooked rice
- 3 tablespoons (42 g) unsalted butter
- 2 teaspoons vanilla
- ¾ cup (175 ml) egg substitute
- 1½ cup (355 ml) evaporated milk
- 2/3 cup (150 g) brown sugar
- ½ teaspoon nutmeg
- 1 cup (145 g) raisins

Directions:

1. Spray slow cooker with nonstick cooking spray. Thoroughly combine all ingredients and pour into prepared slow cooker. Cover and cook on high 2 hours or low 4 to 6 hours. Stir after the first hour.

Nutrition Info:

Per serving: 124 g water; 427 calories (25% from fat, 10% from protein, 65% from carb); 11 g protein; 12 g total fat; 7 g saturated fat; 3 g monounsaturated fat; 1 g polyunsaturated fat; 71 g carb;

1 g fiber; 40 g sugar; 230 mg phosphorus; 224 mg calcium; 2 mg iron; 136 mg sodium; 613 mg potassium; 541 IU vitamin A; 48 mg ATE vitamin E; 2 mg vitamin C; 34 mg cholesterol

Eggs And Sweet Potato Mix

Servings: 4

Cooking Time: 6 Hours And 10 Minutes

Ingredients:

- 2/3 cup sweet potato, grated
- 1 and 1/3 cups leek, chopped
- 2 tablespoons olive oil
- 8 eggs
- 1 cup kale, chopped
- 2 teaspoons garlic, minced
- 1 and ½ cups sausage, chopped

Directions:

1. Heat up a pan with the oil over medium- high heat; add sausage, stir, and brown for 2-3 minutes and transfer to your slow cooker.
2. Add garlic, sweet potatoes, kale and crack the eggs.
3. Stir, cover, cook on Low for 6 hours, divide between plates and serve.

Nutrition Info:

Calories 279, Fat 17.8g, Cholesterol 336mg, Sodium 224mg, Carbohydrate 14g, Fiber 1.9g, Sugars 4g, Protein 14.8g, Potassium 447mg

Rice With Plums

Servings: 4

Cooking Time: 3 Hours

Ingredients:

- 1 cup brown rice
- 2 cups almond milk
- ½ cup plums, pitted and cubed
- 1 tablespoon maple syrup
- 1 teaspoon vanilla extract

Directions:

1. In your slow cooker, combine the rice with the milk and the other ingredients, put the lid on and cook on Low for 3 hours.
2. Divide into bowls and serve for breakfast.

Nutrition Info:

Calories 468, Fat 29.9g, Cholesterol 0mg, Sodium 20mg, Carbohydrate 47.3g, Fiber 4.4g, Sugars 8g, Protein 6.4g, Potassium 468mg

Lemon Bananas

Servings: 4

Cooking Time: 2 Hours

Ingredients:

- 4 bananas, peeled and sliced
- Juice of ½ lemon
- 1 tablespoon coconut oil
- 3 tablespoons stevia
- ½ teaspoon cardamom seeds

Directions:

1. Arrange bananas in your slow cooker, add stevia, lemon juice, oil and cardamom, cover, cook on Low for 2 hours, divide everything into bowls and serve with.

Nutrition Info:

Calories 137, Fat 3.9g, Cholesterol 0mg, Sodium 2mg, Carbohydrate 33.5g, Fiber 3.2g, Sugars 14.6g, Protein 1.4g, Potassium 433mg

Vanilla Grapes Bowls

Servings: 4

Cooking Time: 2 Hours

Ingredients:

- 1 pound green grapes
- 3 tablespoons coconut sugar
- 1 and ½ cups coconut cream
- 2 teaspoons vanilla extract

Directions:

1. In the slow cooker, combine the grapes with the cream and the other ingredients, put the lid on and cook on High for 2 hours.
2. Divide into bowls and serve.

Nutrition Info:

Calories 360, Fat 21.9g, Cholesterol 0mg, Sodium 46mg, Carbohydrate 39g, Fiber 3g, Sugars 21.7g, Protein 3.5g, Potassium 456mg

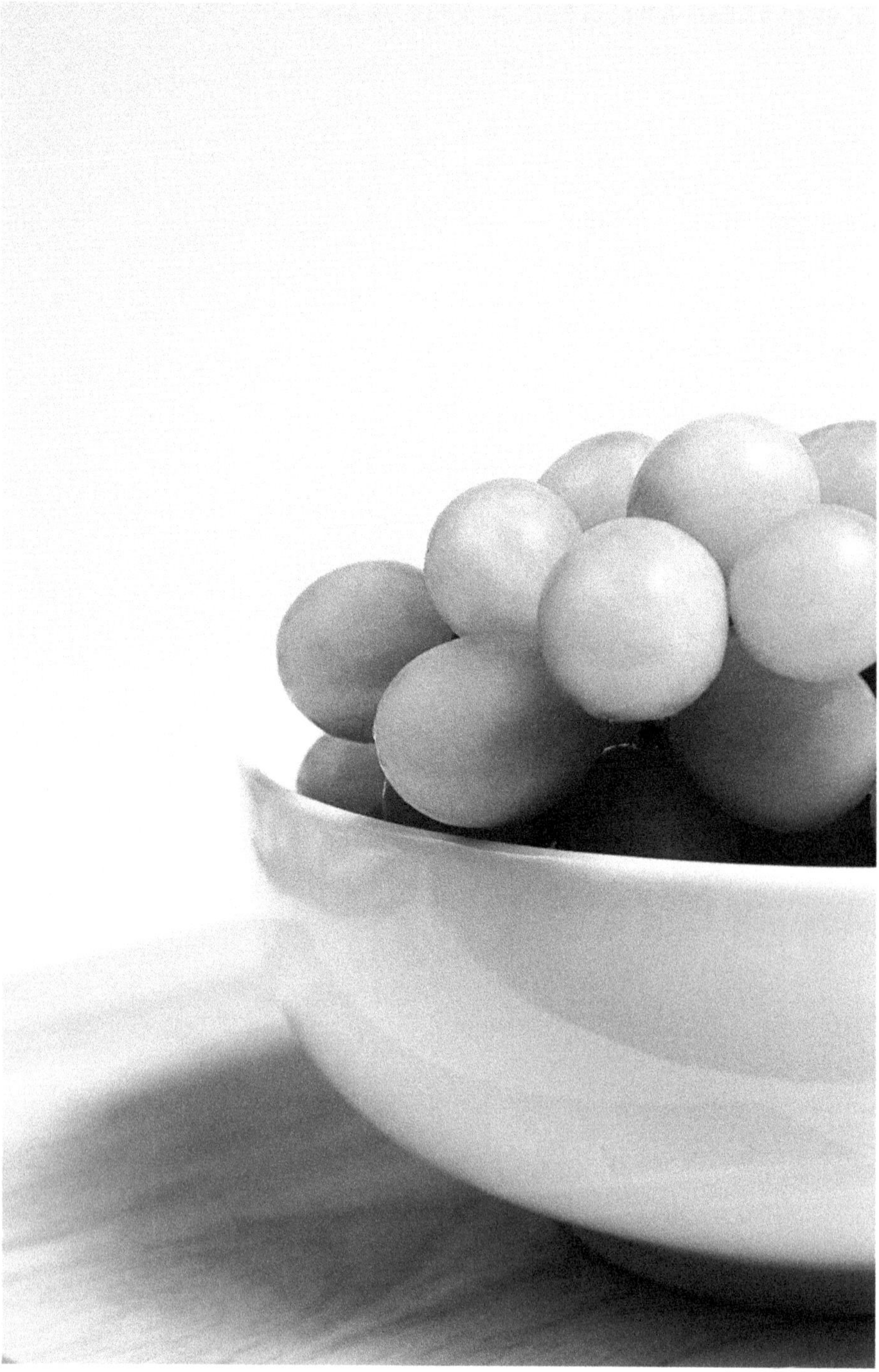

Chives And Cayenne Pepper Omelet

Servings: 4

Cooking Time: 2 Hours

Ingredients:

- 8 eggs, whisked
- 2 ounces low-fat cheddar cheese, grated
- 2 cups spinach, torn
- Cooking spray
- 2 tablespoons chives, chopped
- A pinch of cayenne pepper
- Salt and black pepper to the taste
- For the red pepper relish:
- 2 tablespoons green onion, chopped
- 1 tablespoon vinegar
- 1 cup red pepper, chopped

Directions:

1. In a bowl, mix eggs with salt, pepper, cayenne and chives and stir well.

2. Grease your slow cooker with cooking spray, add eggs mix and spread.

3. Add spinach and cheese, toss, cover and cook on High for 2 hours.

4. In a bowl, mix red pepper with green onions, black pepper to the taste and the vinegar and stir well.

5. Slice the omelet, divide it between plates, top with the relish and serve for breakfast.

Nutrition Info:

Calories 200, Fat 13.8g, Cholesterol 342mg, Sodium 225mg, Carbohydrate 46g, Fiber 0.9g, Sugars 2.4g, Protein 15.4g, Potassium 288mg

Sweet Peanut Butter Rolled Oats

Servings: 2

Cooking Time: 6 Hours

Ingredients:

- 2 tablespoon chia seeds
- 4 tablespoons peanut butter
- 1 cup rolled oats
- 1 cup almond milk
- 1 tablespoon stevia

Directions:

1. In your slow cooker, mix the oats with the milk, chia, peanut butter and stevia, cover and cook on Low for 6 hours.
2. Stir the oats mix, divide into bowls and serve.

Nutrition Info:

Calories 334, Fat 25.5g, Cholesterol 0mg, Sodium 85mg, Carbohydrate 29.9, Fiber 6.1g, Sugars 3.7g, Protein 8.9g, Potassium 356mg

Lemon Zest Pudding

Servings: 4

Cooking Time: 5 Hours

Ingredients:

- 1 cup pineapple juice, natural
- Cooking spray
- 1 teaspoon baking powder
- 1 cup coconut flour
- 3 tablespoons avocado oil
- 3 tablespoons stevia
- ½ cup pineapple, chopped
- ½ cup lemon zest, grated
- ½ cup coconut milk
- ½ cup pecans, chopped

Directions:

1. Spray your slow cooker with cooking spray.
2. In a bowl, mix flour with stevia, baking powder, oil, milk, pecans, pineapple, lemon zest and pineapple juice, stir well, pour into your slow cooker greased with cooking spray, cover and cook on Low for 5 hours.

3. Divide into bowls and serve.

Nutrition Info:

Calories 431, Fat 29.7g, Cholesterol 0mg, Sodium 8mg, Carbohydrate 47.1g, Fiber 17g, Sugars 10.9g, Protein 8.1g, Potassium 482mg

Walnut Apples

Servings: 4

Cooking Time: 2 Hours

Ingredients:

- 1 pound green apples, cored and cut into wedges
- ½ cups coconut cream
- 1 teaspoon cinnamon powder
- 2 tablespoons walnuts, chopped
- 1 tablespoon maple syrup

Directions:

1. In the slow cooker, combine the apples with the cream and the other ingredients, toss, put the lid on and cook on High for 2 hours.
2. Divide into bowls and serve warm.

Nutrition Info:

Calories 135, Fat 9.6g, Cholesterol 0mg, Sodium 6mg, Carbohydrate 13.1g, Fiber 2.3g, Sugars 9.8g, Protein 1.8g, Potassium 169mg

Homemade Granola

Servings: About 5

Cooking Time: 55 Mins

Ingredients:

- 1/8 cup Brown Sugar
- 1 tbsp. Water
- ½ tsp. Vanilla extract
- ½ tbsp. Vegetable Oil
- ½ cup Raisins
- ½ tsp. Cinnamon (ground)
- 2 cups Oats (rolled)
- ¼ cup Milk (low fat)
- ¼ cup Dates (chopped)

Directions:

1. Except for raisins and dates, mix all the ingredients in a bowl.Make sure sugar is thoroughly dissolved.
2. Grease the slow cooker and set it on "High".Cook the granola for 30 mins uncovered.
3. Turn the slow cooker off.
4. Add the raisins and dates and allow the granola to cool. Serve with milk

Nutrition Info:

(Estimated Amount Per Serving): 205 Calories; 5 mg Cholesterol; 440 mg Sodium; 41 mg Carbohydrates; 3 g Dietary Fiber; 7 g Protein

White Fruitcake

Servings: 12 Servings

Ingredients:

- ½ cup (112 g) unsalted butter, softened
- 1 cup (200 g) sugar
- 4 eggs, separated
- 1½ cups (189 g) flour, plus more for coating fruit
- 1½ teaspoons (7 g) baking powder
- 1 cup (225 g) unsweetened crushed pineapple, well drained and juice reserved
- 2/3 cup (160 ml) pineapple juice, drained from crushed pineapple
- 1½ cups (220 g) golden raisins
- 4 ounces (115 g) mixed candied fruit
- 4 ounces (115 g) candied cherries, halved
- 1 cup (110 g) slivered almonds
- ½ teaspoon vanilla extract
- ½ teaspoon almond extract

Directions:

1. Using an electric mixer, cream butter and sugar and then add egg yolks and beat well. Combine flour and

baking powder and add alternately with pineapple juice to butter mixture. Sprinkle flour over raisins and candied fruit and toss to coat. Stir in raisins, candied fruit, crushed pineapple, vanilla, and almond extract, blending thoroughly. Beat egg whites until stiff but not dry; fold into batter. Pour into greased and floured cake pan and cover; place in slow cooker. Pour ½ cup (120 ml) water around cake pan in slow cooker. Cover and steam the fruitcake on high 3 to 5 hours. After baking, allow cake to rest in pan 10 to 15 minutes before removing. Let cool thoroughly before slicing. For mellowing, wrap in plastic wrap when cool.

Nutrition Info:

Per serving: 52 g water; 369 calories (37% from fat, 8% from protein, 55% from carb); 8 g protein; 16 g total fat; 6 g saturated fat; 7 g monounsaturated fat; 2 g polyunsaturated fat; 52 g carb; 3 g fiber; 34 g sugar; 152 mg phosphorus; 90 mg calcium; 2 mg iron; 95 mg sodium; 322 mg potassium; 337 IU vitamin A; 89 mg ATE vitamin E; 4 mg vitamin C; 99 mg cholesterol

Ginger And Pumpkin Pie

Servings: 10

Cooking Time: 2 Hours

Ingredients:

- 2 cups almond flour
- 1 egg, whisked
- 1 cup pumpkin puree
- 1 and ½ teaspoons baking powder
- Cooking spray
- 1 tablespoon coconut oil, melted
- 1 tablespoon vanilla extract
- ½ teaspoon baking soda
- 1 and ½ teaspoons cinnamon powder
- ¼ teaspoon ginger, ground
- 1/3 cup maple syrup
- 1 teaspoon lemon juice

Directions:

1. In a bowl, flour with baking powder, baking soda, cinnamon, ginger, egg, oil, vanilla, pumpkin puree, maple syrup and lemon juice, stir and pour in your slow cooker greased with cooking spray and lined

99

with parchment paper, cover the pot and cook on Low for 2 hours and 20 minutes.

2. Leave the pie to cool down, slice and serve.

Nutrition Info:

Calories 91, Fat 4.8g, Cholesterol 16mg, Sodium 74mg, Carbohydrate 10.8g, Fiber 1.3g, Sugars 7.5g, Protein 2g, Potassium 157mg

Sweet Vanilla Cut Oats

Servings: 4

Cooking Time: 8 Hours

Ingredients:

- 1 cup coconut milk
- 1 cup blueberries
- 2 tablespoons stevia
- ½ teaspoon vanilla extract
- 1 cup steel cut oats
- Coconut flakes for serving
- Cooking spray

Directions:

1. Spray your slow cooker with cooking spray, add oats, milk, stevia, vanilla and blueberries, toss, cover and cook on Low for 8 hours.
2. Divide the oatmeal into bowls, sprinkle coconut flakes on top and serve.

Nutrition Info:

Calories 590, Fat 49.1g, Cholesterol 0mg, Sodium 30mg, Carbohydrate 37.8g, Fiber 13.2g, Sugars 12g, Protein 7.7g, Potassium 614mg

4-WEEK MEAL PLAN

Week 1

Monday
Breakfast: Tofu Frittata
Lunch: Pork Chops In Beer
Dinner: Stewed Tomatoes

Tuesday
Breakfast: Tapioca
Lunch: Creamy Beef Burgundy
Dinner: Oregano Salad

Wednesday
Breakfast: Fruit Oats
Lunch: Smothered Steak
Dinner: Black Beans With Corn Kernels

Thursday
Breakfast: Grapefruit Mix
Lunch: Pork For Sandwiches
Dinner: Stuffed Acorn Squash

Friday
Breakfast: Berry Yogurt
Lunch: Cranberry Pork Roast

Dinner: Greek Eggplant

Saturday
Breakfast: Soft Pudding
Lunch: Pan-asian Pot Roast
Dinner: Thyme Sweet Potatoes

Sunday
Breakfast: Black Beans Salad
Lunch: Short Ribs
Dinner: Barley Vegetable Soup

Week 2

Monday
Breakfast: Carrot Pudding
Lunch: French Dip
Dinner: Butter Corn

Tuesday
Breakfast: Apple Cake
Lunch: Italian Roast With Vegetables
Dinner: Orange Glazed Carrots

Wednesday
Breakfast: Almond Milk Barley Cereals
Lunch: Honey Mustard Ribs
Dinner: Cinnamon Acorn Squash

Thursday

Breakfast: Cashews Cake

Lunch: Pizza Casserole

Dinner: Glazed Root Vegetables

Friday

Breakfast: Artichoke Frittata

Lunch: Hawaiian Pork Roast

Dinner: Stir Fried Steak, Shiitake And Asparagus

Saturday

Breakfast: Mexican Eggs

Lunch: Apple Cranberry Pork Roast

Dinner: Cilantro Brussel Sprouts

Sunday

Breakfast: Stewed Peach

Lunch: Swiss Steak

Dinner: Italian Zucchini

Week 3

Monday

Breakfast: Lamb Cassoule t

Lunch: Glazed Pork Roast

Dinner: Cilantro Parsnip Chunks

Tuesday

Breakfast: Fruited Tapioca

Lunch: Swiss Steak In Wine Sauce

Dinner: Corn Casserole

Wednesday

Breakfast: Baby Spinach Shrimp Salad

Lunch: Italian Pork Chops

Dinner: Pilaf With Bella Mushrooms

Thursday

Breakfast: Coconut And Fruit Cake

Lunch: Italian Pot Roast

Dinner: Italian Style Yellow Squash

Friday

Breakfast: Apple And Squash Bowls

Lunch: Beef With Horseradish Sauce

Dinner: Stevia Peas With Marjoram

Saturday

Breakfast: Slow Cooker Chocolate Cake

Lunch: Oriental Pot Roast

Dinner: Broccoli Rice Casserole

Sunday

Breakfast: Fish Omelet

Lunch: Barbecued Ribs

Dinner: Italians Style Mushroom Mix

Week 4

Monday
Breakfast: Brown Cake
Lunch: Ham And Scalloped Pota toes
Dinner: Broccoli Casserole

Tuesday
Breakfast: Stevia And Walnuts Cut Oats
Lunch: Pork And Pineapple Roast

Wednesday
Breakfast: Walnut And Cinnamon Oatmeal
Lunch: Barbecued Brisket
Dinner: Dinner: Slow Cooker Lasagna

Thursday
Breakfast: Tender Rosemary Sweet Potatoes
Lunch: Barbecued Short Ribs
Dinner: Brussels Sprouts Casserole

Friday
Breakfast: Orange And Maple Syrup Quinoa
Lunch: Beer-braised Short Ribs
Dinner: Pasta And Mushrooms

Saturday
Breakfast: Vanilla And Nutmeg Oatmeal
Lunch: Lamb Stew
Dinner: Onion Cabbage

Sunday

Breakfast: Pecans Cake

Lunch: Barbecued Ham

Dinner: Cheese Broccoli

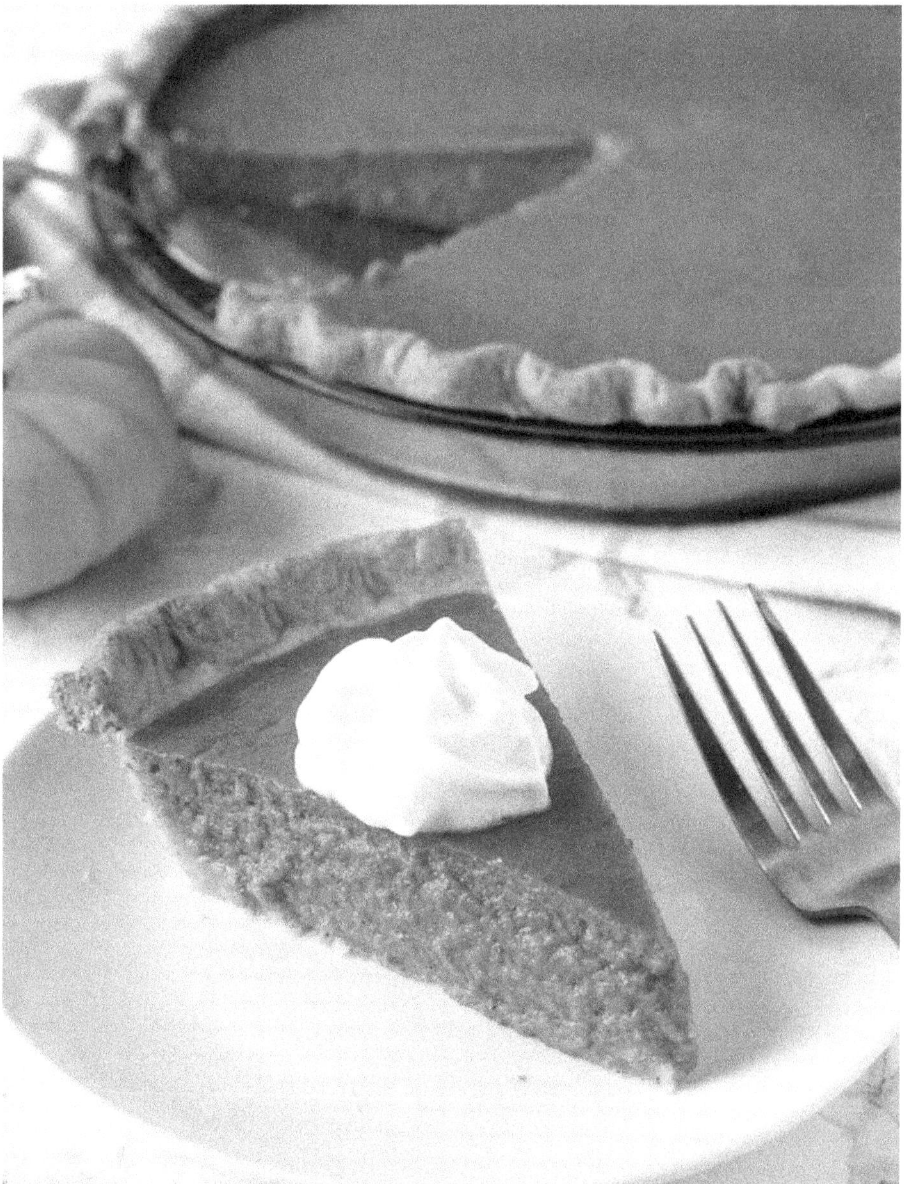

Lightning Source UK Ltd.
Milton Keynes UK
UKHW050828291222
414375UK00005B/32